DINOSAURS RULED!

STEGOSAURUS

Leigh Rockwood

PowerKiDS press

New York

Published in 2012 by The Rosen Publishing Group, Inc.
29 East 21st Street, New York, NY 10010

First Edition

Editor: Joanne Randolph
Book Design: Kate Laczynski

Photo Credits: Cover, title page by Brian Garvey; cover background (palm tree leaves) © www.iStockphoto.com/dra_schwartz; cover background (palm tree trunk) iStockphoto/Thinkstock; cover background (ginkgo leaves) Hemera/Thinkstock; cover background (fern leaves) Brand X Pictures/Thinkstock; cover background (moss texture) © www.iStockphoto.com/Robert Linton; pp. 4–5, 7, 9, 10–11, 12, 13 (left), 14–15, 16 (left), 18–19, 19 (top), 20, 21, 22 © 2011 Orpheus Books Ltd.; pp. 6, 8 Shutterstock.com; p. 13 (right) © www.iStockphoto.com/Steve Brigman; pp. 16–17 © www.iStockphoto.com/SPrada; p. 17 (right) Jupiterimages/Photos.com/Thinkstock.

Library of Congress Cataloging-in-Publication Data

Rockwood, Leigh.
  Stegosaurus / by Leigh Rockwood. — 1st ed.
      p. cm. — (Dinosaurs ruled!)
  Includes index.
  ISBN 978-1-4488-4963-5 (library binding) — ISBN 978-1-4488-5076-1 (pbk.) —
ISBN 978-1-4488-5077-8 (6-pack)
  1. Stegosaurus—Juvenile literature. I. Title. II. Series.
  QE862.O65R625 2012
  567.915'3—dc22

                                    2010047569

Manufactured in the United States of America

CPSIA Compliance Information: Batch #WS11PK: For Further Information contact Rosen Publishing, New York, New York at 1-800-237-9932

CONTENTS

MEET THE STEGOSAURUS

The stegosaurus was a dinosaur that knew how to stand out in a crowd. It had a spiked tail that it could swing around to fight off its enemies. It is best known for the thin, bony plates that stood up along its back. In fact, the stegosaurus got its name from those plates. "Stegosaurus" means "roofed lizard."

Paleontologists study stegosaurus **fossils** to learn more about these dinosaurs. Everything they find helps them come up with new theories, or ideas, about how stegosauruses lived. Fossils also give paleontologists ideas about why these dinosaurs became **extinct**.

The stegosaurus is one of the most easily recognized dinosaurs. It is known for the plates on its back and its tail spikes.

5

THE LATE JURASSIC PERIOD

Paleontologists use a system called geologic time to talk about Earth's long history. The stegosaurus lived during the Late Jurassic period. The Late Jurassic period was the time from about 160 to 145 million years ago. At the beginning of the Jurassic period, the continents as we know them today were a giant landmass called Pangaea. By the Late Jurassic period, Pangaea had begun to break apart.

The Jurassic period gets its name from the Jura Mountains. These mountains lie in France and Switzerland.

Here are some of the other dinosaurs and giant reptiles that lived around the same time as the stegosaurus. The person in this picture gives you a sense of the dinosaur's size.

The **climate** was warm during the Late Jurassic period. Large trees, such as **conifers**, were plentiful. These trees fed plant-eating dinosaurs, such as the stegosaurus. Meat-eating dinosaurs, such as the allosaurus, hunted and ate plant-eating dinosaurs.

WHERE DID STEGOSAURUSES LIVE?

Did you know that the land that is now the United States had more different kinds of dinosaurs than any other place on Earth? Many dinosaur fossils were found in the Morrison Formation. This is a group of **sedimentary rock** formations in the western United States. There are many fossils in these rock formations, including the remains of stegosauruses.

DINO BITE

Sedimentary rocks form when small bits of sand, stone, or mud are deposited somewhere. This matter is called sediment. Over time the sediment gets pressed together and becomes rock. Sometimes a dead plant or animal is trapped in the sediment. These dead plants or animals can form fossils as the sediment hardens into rock.

The stegosaurus and its relatives, along with many other dinosaurs, lived in a habitat with trees, ferns, and other plants. Today the places where they lived are mostly rocky desert.

Stegosaurus fossils have been found in the Morrison Formation in Wyoming, Utah, and Colorado. During the Late Jurassic period, these places were likely wet, wooded, and full of plant life. Stegosaurus fossils have been found in India, China, and Africa, too.

THE STEGOSAURUS BODY

A full-grown stegosaurus was about 26 feet (8 m) long. It stood about 21 feet (6 m) tall and weighed about 2 to 3 tons (2–3 t). Its head was about the size of a horse's head. A head that size looked small on such a big body!

The stegosaurus walked on four thick, elephant-like legs. Its back

Here you can see the stegosaurus's tiny head and longer back legs.

legs were longer than its front legs. This meant that its back made a curved shape. It had a spiky tail that it might have used to fight off **predators**. What really made the stegosaurus stand out from other dinosaurs were the two rows of plates along its back.

WHAT ABOUT THOSE PLATES?

DINO BITE

Some paleontologists think that the skin on the stegosaurus's plates might have been brightly colored and used to draw mates to them.

The stegosaurus had 17 thin, bony plates along its back. These plates were in two rows. The largest of a stegosaurus's plates was generally about 2.5 feet (76 cm) tall.

Paleontologists have had many theories about why the stegosaurus had plates. They do not think the

Paleontologists think the stegosaurus's plates looked like this dinosaur's shown here.

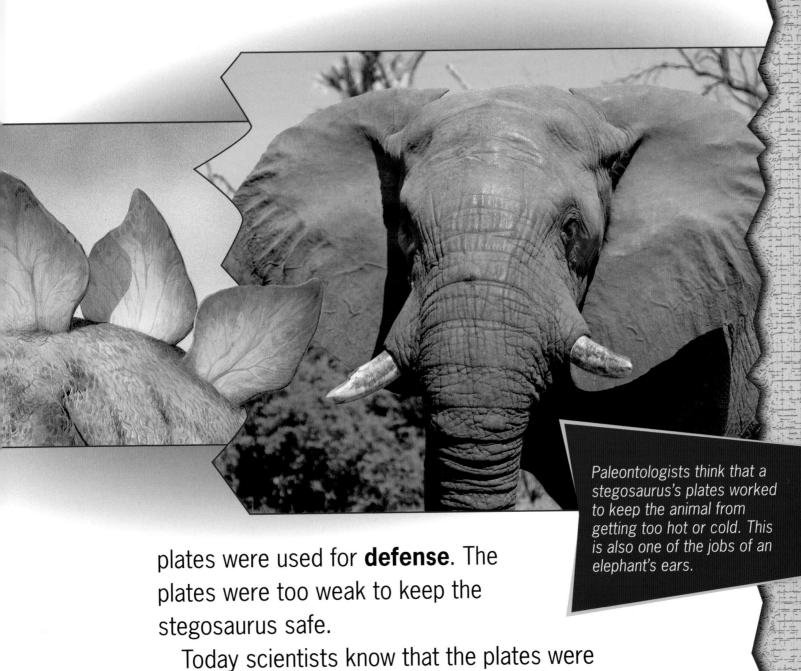

Paleontologists think that a stegosaurus's plates worked to keep the animal from getting too hot or cold. This is also one of the jobs of an elephant's ears.

plates were used for **defense**. The plates were too weak to keep the stegosaurus safe.

Today scientists know that the plates were covered with skin. They think that the plates helped the dinosaur control its body temperature. The plates could have either let out body heat or helped the stegosaurus warm up while sitting in the sun.

BIG BODY, TINY BRAIN

The stegosaurus had a small head compared with the size of its body. The brain inside its horse-sized skull was only about the size of a walnut. The stegosaurus's brain was much smaller than that of other dinosaurs. Because of this, paleontologists think that the stegosaurus was not very smart. They think it was far less smart than other dinosaurs of the Late Jurassic period.

The stegosaurus was about the size of a bus. It was smaller than many other dinosaurs, though. Do you see how small its head is compared with these other dinosaurs, too?

Paleontologists once thought that the stegosaurus might have had a second brain near the hips, which controlled its back legs and tail. Today scientists know that that was not the case. The stegosaurus was a big dinosaur with a tiny brain!

A PLANT-EATING DINOSAUR

The stegosaurus ate only leaves and small plants. Scientists do not think it had a strong enough jaw to eat larger branches or hard plant matter.

The stegosaurus was an **herbivore**. This means it ate plants. It had a beaklike mouth, which it used to tear leaves from plants. Stegosauruses had small, ridged teeth that ground up the leaves.

The stegosaurus's diet was most likely made up of plants. These might have included mosses, ferns, horsetails, and conifers. These are all plants that

Cycads were common in the Late Jurassic period, when the stegosaurus lived. The stegosaurus likely ate cycad leaves and seeds as part of its diet.

Horsetails were an important food for plant-eating dinosaurs, including the stegosaurus. These plants are still around today.

were plentiful in the Late Jurassic period. They were also plentiful in places where stegosaurus fossils have been found.

The stegosaurus was a really big dinosaur. It would have had to eat a lot every day to stay alive. It likely spent most of its time looking for food.

SAFETY IN NUMBERS?

Paleontologists think that the stegosaurus lived in herds or came together in groups to feed. Other plant-eating dinosaurs, such as the diplodocus, are thought to have traveled in herds, too. A group of

Paleontologists found tracks that tell them that the stegosaurus likely lived in multiage groups.

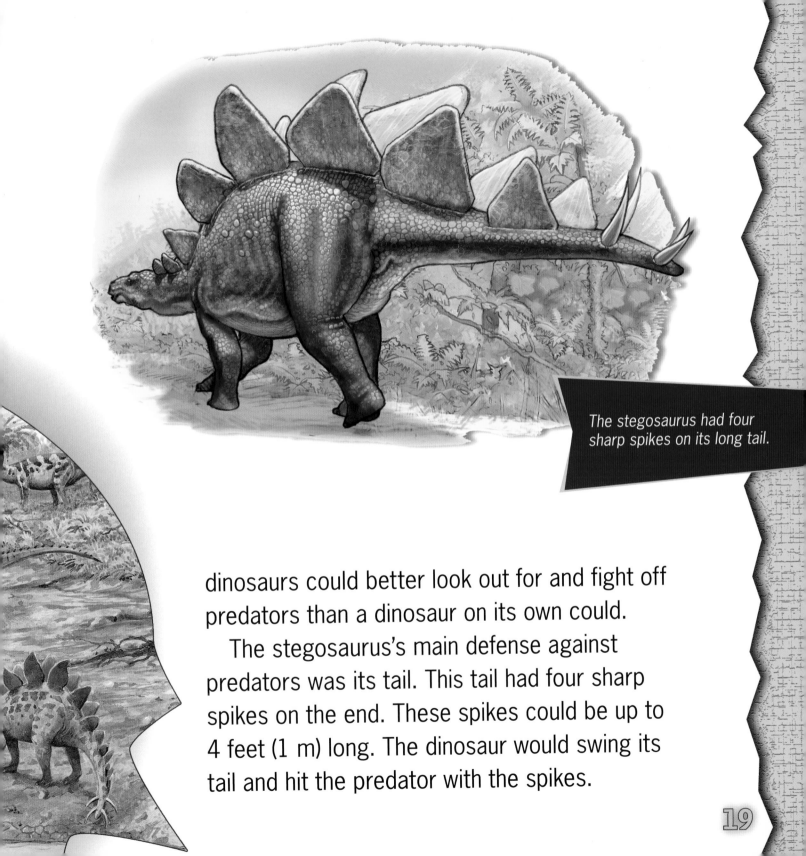

The stegosaurus had four sharp spikes on its long tail.

dinosaurs could better look out for and fight off predators than a dinosaur on its own could.

The stegosaurus's main defense against predators was its tail. This tail had four sharp spikes on the end. These spikes could be up to 4 feet (1 m) long. The dinosaur would swing its tail and hit the predator with the spikes.

STEGOSAURUS PREDATORS

DINO BITE

A stegosaurus's plates are much like the bumps on a crocodile's back, just bigger! The plates were not fixed to the skeleton. Instead they were part of the skin.

Paleontologists think that the stegosaurus was likely a slow-moving dinosaur. They think this because its front and back legs were different lengths. Its slow pace would have made it appealing to nearby **carnivorous**, or meat-eating, dinosaurs. Carnivorous dinosaurs that lived in the same places as the stegosaurus included the allosaurus, ceratosaurus, marshosaurus, torvosaurus, and ornitholestes.

A blow from the stegosaurus's spiked tail would have sent many a hungry predator in search of easier prey.

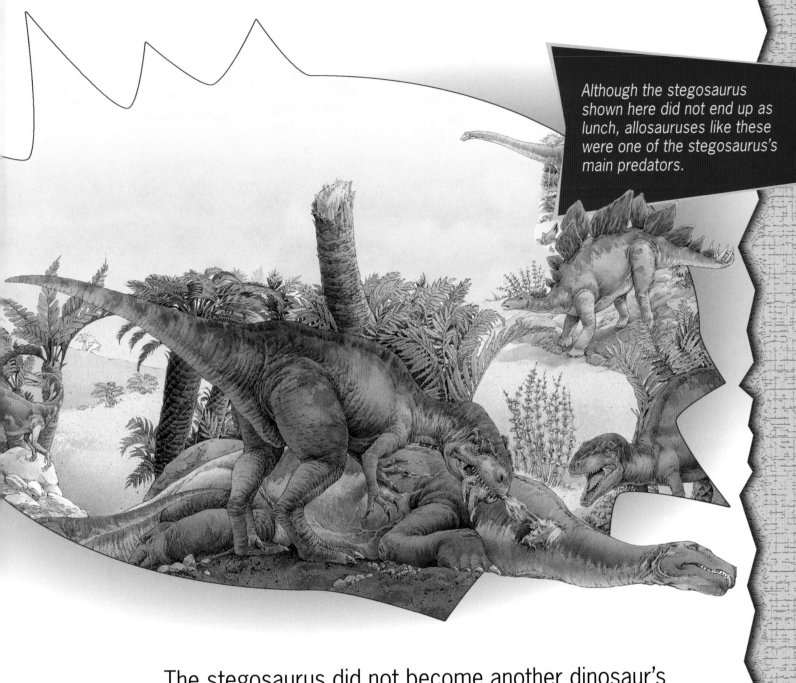

Although the stegosaurus shown here did not end up as lunch, allosauruses like these were one of the stegosaurus's main predators.

The stegosaurus did not become another dinosaur's dinner without a fight, though. Paleontologists have found an allosaurus backbone that has a spike-shaped hole in it that likely came from a stegosaurus's tail!

NO BONES ABOUT IT

You may wonder how we know about an animal that lived so long ago. Rancher Marshall Felch found the first stegosaurus fossils in 1876. Paleontologist Othniel Marsh led the dig in the rock quarry on Felch's ranch. He is the person who gave the stegosaurus its name.

Thanks to the work of paleontologists, we know a lot about dinosaurs. What else do you want to know about the stegosaurus?

Paleontologists carefully remove fossilized remains from the rock and dirt in which they are found. Every time new fossils are found it is a chance for scientists to learn new things or to change earlier ideas about that dinosaur. Even though stegosauruses became extinct millions of years ago, there are plenty of discoveries still to be made.

GLOSSARY

carnivorous (kahr-NIH-vuh-rus) Eating animals.

climate (KLY-mut) The kind of weather a certain place has.

conifers (KAH-nih-furz) Trees that have needlelike leaves and grow cones.

defense (dih-FENTS) Something a living thing does that helps keep it safe.

extinct (ek-STINGKT) No longer existing.

fossils (FO-sulz) Hardened remains of dead animals or plants.

herbivore (ER-buh-vor) An animal that eats plants.

paleontologists (pay-lee-on-TAH-luh-jists) People who study things that lived in the past.

predators (PREH-duh-terz) Animals that kill other animals for food.

sedimentary rock (seh-deh-MEN-teh-ree ROK) Stones, sand, or mud that has been pressed together to form rock.

INDEX

WEB SITES

Due to the changing nature of Internet links, PowerKids Press has developed an online list of Web sites related to the subject of this book. This site is updated regularly. Please use this link to access the list:

www.powerkidslinks.com/dinr/stego/